Soaring to Success
in Business & Leadership

Swifter, Higher, Stronger!

Gerard Assey

Soaring to Success
in Business & Leadership
Swifter, Higher, Stronger!
By
Gerard Assey

Published by:
Gerard Assey
19/18, Palli Arasan Street
Anna Nagar East
Chennai - 600 102

ISBN: 978-93-92492-99-0

(Image courtesy Freepik: 'https://www.freepik.com' Thank You)

Table of Contents

Preface

In the world of business and leadership, the pursuit of excellence and success is an ongoing journey, one that demands continuous growth and adaptation. The eagle, with its remarkable qualities of swiftness, height, and strength, serves as a compelling symbol for those who seek to excel in life. This book, **'Soaring to Success in Business & Leadership: Swifter, Higher, Stronger!'** is a testament to the idea that nature can be a profound teacher, and the majestic eagle, a great guide.

In the following chapters, we embark on a journey of exploration and discovery, drawing inspiration from the eagle's extraordinary traits and behaviors. As we delve into the world of eagles, we uncover lessons that extend far beyond the realm of ornithology, offering profound insights into how we can lead, excel, and triumph in the intricate dance of business and leadership.

Each chapter of this book is dedicated to a specific trait exhibited by eagles, and the lessons derived from their behavior are illuminated through real-world examples, actionable strategies, and the guidance needed to cultivate these traits in our own lives. From visionary leadership to teamwork, from persistence to resilience, from embracing failure to leading by example, these lessons are designed to empower individuals in their personal and professional quests.

But this book is more than just a manual for leadership and personal growth. It's a tribute to the beauty and wisdom of nature, a reminder that the natural world is a vast repository of lessons waiting to be uncovered. The eagle, as our guide and inspiration, reminds us of the boundless potential within ourselves, urging us to reach new heights and strive for excellence.

As you embark on this journey, open your mind to the wisdom of the eagle, and let its lessons inspire you to become the leader you aspire to be. Whether you're an experienced executive, an aspiring entrepreneur, or simply someone seeking personal growth and fulfillment, the wisdom of the eagle can help you soar to new heights and achieve remarkable success.

So, let us spread our wings and embark on this soaring journey together. As we learn from the eagle and apply these lessons to our lives, may we find the courage to chase our dreams, the wisdom to navigate the storms, and the strength to reach new heights in both our professional and personal endeavors.

Welcome to **'Soaring to Success in Business & Leadership: Swifter, Higher, Stronger!'**

Swifter, Higher, Stronger!

In the vast landscape of business and leadership, individuals and organizations constantly strive for excellence and success. It's a realm filled with challenges, opportunities, and the need to constantly evolve. Within this dynamic environment, we can draw inspiration from the eagle, a magnificent creature that embodies qualities of swiftness, height, and strength. The eagle's remarkable traits are not just symbolic; they offer profound lessons that can guide us in our pursuit of greatness, not only in business but in every facet of life.

Swiftness, Height, and Strength as Metaphors

1. Swiftness: The eagle's swiftness in hunting and navigating the skies reminds us of the importance of swift decision-making in the business world. Just as an eagle seizes its prey with precision, business leaders must make timely decisions to capitalize on opportunities and avoid pitfalls.

Example: Consider the story of Steve Jobs, who was known for his swift decision-making at Apple. When he returned to the company in 1997, he promptly reduced the product lineup, focusing on a few key products, leading to Apple's resurgence.

Action Plan:

- ✓ Identify areas in your decision-making process that can be streamlined.
- ✓ Develop a system for gathering relevant information quickly.
- ✓ Trust your instincts when time is of the essence, but ensure they are informed by data.

2. Height: Eagles soar to great heights, providing them with a broad perspective of the landscape below. Similarly, visionary leaders possess the ability to see beyond immediate challenges and envision a brighter future.

Example: Elon Musk, with his ambitious projects like SpaceX and Tesla, exemplifies visionary leadership by aiming for a future where humanity colonizes other planets and transitions to sustainable energy.

Action Plan:

- ✓ Cultivate the habit of looking beyond short-term goals to envision a long-term vision.
- ✓ Communicate your vision clearly to inspire and align your team.
- ✓ Encourage creative thinking and innovation to realize your vision.

3. Strength: Eagles are known for their immense strength, which they use not only for hunting but also to endure challenging conditions. In leadership and life, strength manifests as resilience, adaptability, and the ability to persevere in the face of adversity.

Example: Nelson Mandela's strength during his long imprisonment and his commitment to reconciliation after his release demonstrate unparalleled resilience and strength of character.

Action Plan:

- ✓ Develop resilience by learning from setbacks and using them as stepping stones.
- ✓ Embrace change and adapt swiftly to evolving circumstances.
- ✓ Cultivate the mental and emotional fortitude to persevere through tough times.

The Journey Ahead

'Soaring to Success in Business & Leadership: Swifter, Higher, Stronger!' is not just a book; it's a transformative journey. In the chapters that follow, we will delve deeper into each of these eagle-inspired qualities, exploring real-life examples, and providing actionable strategies to develop these traits. By understanding and integrating the principles of swiftness, height, and strength into our lives and organizations, we can aspire to achieve greatness and soar to new heights of success.

Why is it important for Business Leaders to Work on these Traits? The Benefits & Repercussions

Business leaders should work on developing these traits because these traits are essential for effective leadership and can lead to numerous benefits for both the leaders themselves and their organizations. Failing to cultivate these traits can have negative repercussions. Here's a list of the benefits of developing these traits and the repercussions of neglecting them, along with examples:

1. Visionary Leadership:

- ✓ **Benefits:** Visionary leaders inspire and motivate their teams, drive innovation, and create a sense of purpose. They can lead organizations to long-term success.
- ✓ **Repercussions:** Without a clear vision, leaders may struggle to provide direction, leading to confusion and lack of motivation among employees.
- ✓ *Example:* Steve Jobs' visionary leadership at Apple led to groundbreaking products like the iPhone, which transformed the company and the entire smartphone industry.

2. Teamwork:

- ✓ **Benefits:** Effective teamwork improves productivity, creativity, and employee satisfaction. It enhances collaboration and helps organizations achieve their goals.
- ✓ **Repercussions:** A lack of teamwork can result in silos, communication breakdowns, and inefficiencies within an organization.

- ✓ *Example:* Google's successful projects often involve cross-functional teams collaborating to develop innovative solutions.

3. **Persistence:**
   - ✓ **Benefits:** Persistent leaders persevere through challenges, inspiring resilience in their teams. They are more likely to overcome obstacles and achieve their goals.
   - ✓ **Repercussions:** Leaders who give up easily in the face of adversity can demotivate their teams and hinder progress.
   - ✓ *Example:* Thomas Edison's persistence in inventing the light bulb involved thousands of failed attempts before success.
4. **Resilience:**
   - ✓ **Benefits:** Resilient leaders can handle stress, setbacks, and uncertainty effectively. They bounce back from failures and maintain a positive work environment.
   - ✓ **Repercussions:** Leaders who lack resilience may crumble under pressure, affecting decision-making and team morale.
   - ✓ *Example:* Nelson Mandela's resilience during his imprisonment allowed him to lead South Africa's transition to democracy.
5. **Embracing Failure:**
   - ✓ **Benefits:** Leaders who embrace failure as a learning opportunity foster innovation and personal growth. They are more adaptable and willing to take calculated risks.
   - ✓ **Repercussions:** Fear of failure can stifle creativity, hinder decision-making, and prevent organizations from seizing opportunities.

- ✓ *Example:* Amazon's willingness to experiment and accept failure has led to innovations like the Kindle and Amazon Web Services.

6. Leadership by Example:

- ✓ **Benefits:** Leaders who lead by example build trust, credibility, and respect among their teams. They inspire employees to follow their values and work ethic.
- ✓ **Repercussions:** Leaders who do not practice what they preach may face resistance from their teams and undermine organizational culture.
- ✓ *Example:* Mahatma Gandhi's commitment to nonviolent resistance inspired millions and influenced India's independence movement.

In summary, developing these traits is crucial for business leaders because they contribute to effective leadership, employee engagement, innovation, and long-term organizational success. Neglecting these traits can result in confusion, de-motivation, inefficiency, and missed opportunities, ultimately hindering an organization's growth and competitiveness in the market.

Assess Your Levels of these Traits- Before & After Reading the Book

Assessing a leader's proficiency in the areas covered in the book both before and after reading and implementing its lessons is essential for gauging personal growth and improvement. Below, I provide a detailed assessment and evaluation system for before and after:

Before Reading the Book Assessment:

Self-Reflection Questionnaire:

Develop a questionnaire covering key traits and behaviors discussed in the book. Leaders can self-assess their current proficiency in each area.

Sample questions for each trait:

- ✓ Visionary Leadership: "How well-defined is my personal and organizational vision?"
- ✓ Teamwork: "How effectively do I promote collaboration within my team or organization?"
- ✓ Persistence: "Do I often give up on goals when faced with challenges?"
- ✓ Resilience: "How well do I handle stress and setbacks?"
- ✓ Embracing Failure: "Do I view failure as a learning opportunity or as a setback?"
- ✓ Leadership by Example: "Am I consistently modeling the behavior I expect from my team?"

360-Degree Feedback:

- ✓ Seek feedback from peers, superiors, and subordinates to gather insights into your leadership strengths and weaknesses.
- ✓ Use anonymous surveys or interviews to encourage honest feedback.

Goal Setting:

- ✓ Establish specific, measurable goals for improvement in each trait.
- ✓ Outline the desired changes you want to make based on your self-assessment and feedback.

After Reading the Book and Implementing Lessons Assessment:

Self-Reflection Reassessment:

- ✓ Re-administer the self-assessment questionnaire to evaluate changes in your proficiency in each trait.
- ✓ Compare your scores before and after reading the book to identify areas of improvement.

360-Degree Feedback Reassessment:

- ✓ Collect feedback from the same group of peers, superiors, and subordinates to measure changes in perceptions of your leadership.

Goal Progress Evaluation:

- ✓ Review the goals you set before reading the book.
- ✓ Assess the extent to which you have achieved these goals.
- ✓ Note any specific examples or instances where you applied lessons from the book successfully.

Behavioral Observations:

- ✓ Document instances of specific behaviors or actions that reflect improvements in the targeted traits.
- ✓ Provide concrete examples of how you have demonstrated each trait in your leadership role.

Assessment Metrics:

For each trait, consider using a scale (e.g., 1-5) or descriptive language to measure progress:

- ✓ **Visionary Leadership:** Measure improvements in the clarity and alignment of your vision, and your ability to inspire and communicate it.
- ✓ **Teamwork:** Evaluate changes in the level of collaboration, communication, and empowerment within your team.
- ✓ **Persistence:** Assess whether you are now setting and achieving more challenging goals and persevering in the face of obstacles.
- ✓ **Resilience:** Measure your improved ability to handle stress, bounce back from setbacks, and maintain a positive outlook.
- ✓ **Embracing Failure:** Evaluate your attitude toward failure and your willingness to take calculated risks.
- ✓ **Leadership by Example:** Assess your consistency in modeling desired behaviors and the impact on your team's morale and performance.

Tracking Progress:

- ✓ Maintain a journal or digital record to document your personal reflections, feedback received, and instances of improvement.
- ✓ Periodically review and analyze this record to track your progress over time.

Feedback Loop:

- ✓ Continuously seek feedback and assess your leadership qualities at regular intervals (e.g., every six months) to ensure ongoing growth and development.

By implementing this assessment and evaluation system, leaders can gain valuable insights into their growth and development in these crucial leadership traits both before and after reading the book. It provides a structured approach to measuring progress and encourages a commitment to continuous improvement in leadership effectiveness.

Chapter 1:
The Art of Precision - Swiftness

Lesson 1 - Swift Decision-Making

Importance of Making Quick but Well-Informed Decisions

In the fast-paced world of business and leadership, one of the most critical skills is the ability to make swift decisions. While it's essential to act promptly, decisions must also be well-informed to ensure their effectiveness. Swift decision-making is akin to the eagle's precision when it dives to capture its prey. Here, we will explore the significance of this trait, draw inspiration from leaders who have excelled due to their quick thinking, and provide actionable strategies to cultivate and enhance this skill.

Swift Decision-Making in Business and Leadership

Swift decision-making is crucial for several reasons:

- ✓ Seizing Opportunities: In today's competitive landscape, opportunities come and go quickly. Leaders who can make decisions swiftly are more likely to capitalize on these opportunities and gain a competitive edge.
- ✓ Crisis Management: During crises, such as market disruptions or unexpected challenges, quick decisions can be the difference between survival and failure. Leaders who can act promptly can steer their organizations through turbulent times.
- ✓ Adapting to Change: The business environment is constantly evolving. Swift decision-makers can adapt more effectively to changing circumstances and stay ahead of the curve.

Examples of Leaders Excelling in Swift Decision-Making

***Example 1**: Jeff Bezos (Amazon):* Jeff Bezos, the founder of Amazon, is renowned for his ability to make rapid decisions. Amazon's success can be attributed, in part, to Bezos's willingness to act swiftly in expanding the company's product and service offerings. For instance, Amazon Prime was conceived and launched within a short timeframe, revolutionizing the e-commerce industry.

***Example 2:** Indra Nooyi (Former CEO of PepsiCo):* Indra Nooyi, during her tenure as CEO of PepsiCo, demonstrated swift decision-making in restructuring the company's product portfolio to focus on healthier options. Her ability to pivot the company towards health-conscious consumers was instrumental in its sustained growth.

Action Plan: Strategies to Improve Decision-Making Speed without Sacrificing Quality

Prioritize Information Gathering:

- ✓ Gather relevant data and insights before making decisions.
- ✓ Distinguish between critical information and extraneous details to avoid analysis paralysis.

Set Decision-Making Timelines:

- ✓ Establish deadlines for decisions to prevent procrastination.
- ✓ Use techniques like the "2-Minute Rule" for quick, straightforward decisions.

Trust Your Intuition:

- ✓ Cultivate your instincts through experience and learning.

- ✓ Use your intuition as a complementary tool when time is limited.

Delegate and Empower:

- ✓ Empower your team to make decisions within their areas of expertise.
- ✓ Create a culture where employees feel confident making choices without constant approval.

Continuous Learning:

- ✓ Stay informed about industry trends and best practices.
- ✓ Regularly evaluate and learn from past decisions to refine your decision-making process.

Mental Preparedness:

- ✓ Train your mind to process information quickly by practicing mindfulness and meditation.
- ✓ Maintain mental clarity and focus to make decisions under pressure.

It's your turn! Put this into real action now!

Exercise 1: Decision Journal

- ✓ Create a decision journal to track your daily decisions.
- ✓ For each decision, note the options considered, the rationale behind your choice, and the outcomes.
- ✓ Reflect on whether you could have made any decisions more swiftly without sacrificing quality.
- ✓ Set a goal to make at least one quicker but well-informed decision each day for a week.

By honing your swift decision-making skills, you can navigate the dynamic landscape of business and leadership with agility and effectiveness. Just like the eagle swoops down with precision to secure its prey, you too can seize opportunities and overcome challenges swiftly, all while ensuring the quality and impact of your decisions.

Lesson 2 - Adaptability

Understanding Adaptability: Learning from Eagles

Adaptability is a hallmark of success in both the natural world and the realm of business and leadership. Eagles, as masters of adaptation, provide us with valuable lessons on how to thrive in changing conditions. In this lesson, we'll delve into the remarkable ways eagles adapt to evolving circumstances, examine real-world examples of businesses and individuals who have thrived due to their adaptability, and provide actionable strategies to enhance your adaptability in a dynamic environment.

How Eagles Adapt to Changing Conditions

Eagles' ability to adapt to diverse situations is evident in their hunting and soaring behaviors:

1. Hunting Tactics: Eagles exhibit a range of hunting techniques, adapting to the type and behavior of their prey. For example, they may dive swiftly to catch fish or engage in aerial acrobatics when pursuing agile birds.
2. Environmental Awareness: Eagles are highly attuned to changes in weather and terrain. They adjust their flight patterns and hunting grounds accordingly, optimizing their chances of success.
3. Resourcefulness: Eagles are opportunistic feeders. They adapt their diet to what is available in their surroundings, ensuring they have sustenance in varying conditions.

Real-World Stories of Adaptability

Example 1: *Netflix:* Netflix began as a DVD rental service but adapted to the digital age by transitioning into a streaming platform. Their ability to pivot and cater to changing consumer preferences revolutionized the entertainment industry and led to their dominance in the streaming market.

Example 2: *Amazon:* Amazon, founded by Jeff Bezos in 1994 as an online bookstore, initially focused on selling books. However, Bezos demonstrated exceptional adaptability as he recognized the potential of e-commerce and rapidly expanded the company's offerings. Over the years, Amazon evolved into a global e-commerce giant, offering a wide range of products, services, and technology solutions.

Lessons from Amazon's Adaptability:

- ✓ **Customer-Centric Approach**: Amazon's adaptability is rooted in its commitment to customer satisfaction. They continuously gather customer feedback and adapt their offerings and services to meet evolving consumer needs and preferences.
- ✓ **Innovation and Diversification**: Amazon's adaptability is evident in its diversification into various sectors, including cloud computing (Amazon Web Services), digital streaming (Amazon Prime Video), and smart devices (Amazon Echo). This diversification allows the company to thrive in different market conditions.
- ✓ **Agility and Risk-Taking**: Amazon embraces an agile culture that encourages experimentation and risk-taking. They are willing to invest in new ventures and

technologies, even if they don't immediately yield profits, recognizing that long-term adaptability and growth often require short-term sacrifices.

- ✓ **Technological Advancements**: Amazon is at the forefront of technological innovation, using data-driven insights and cutting-edge technology to optimize its operations and enhance the customer experience. This adaptability in adopting new technologies keeps the company competitive.

By examining Amazon's journey from an online bookstore to a global e-commerce and technology giant, we see a remarkable demonstration of adaptability in the business world. Jeff Bezos's ability to pivot and evolve the company's strategies based on changing market dynamics and customer demands underscores the importance of adaptability in achieving sustained success.

Action Plan: Techniques to Enhance Your Adaptability in a Dynamic Environment

Embrace Change as Opportunity:

- ✓ Develop a mindset that views change as a chance for growth and improvement.
- ✓ Encourage your team to see challenges as learning experiences.

Continuous Learning and Skill Development:

- ✓ Stay up-to-date with industry trends and acquire new skills.
- ✓ Invest in ongoing training and development for yourself and your team.

Flexibility in Strategy:

- ✓ Be open to adjusting your strategies and tactics as circumstances change.
- ✓ Maintain a portfolio of options to adapt to different scenarios.

Environmental Scanning:

- ✓ Regularly assess your external environment, including market conditions and customer preferences.
- ✓ Use data and market research to inform your decisions and adapt proactively.

Cultivate Resilience:

- ✓ Build emotional resilience to handle the stress and uncertainty that often accompanies change.
- ✓ Foster a supportive workplace culture that helps employees cope with change.

Feedback and Iteration:

- ✓ Solicit feedback from colleagues, mentors, and customers to identify areas for improvement.
- ✓ Use feedback to iterate and refine your strategies and products.

It's your turn! Put this into real action now!

Exercise 2: Change Scenario Analysis

- ✓ Identify a recent change or challenge in your work environment.
- ✓ List the specific ways in which you adapted to the situation.
- ✓ Reflect on how your adaptability influenced the outcome.
- ✓ Develop a plan for proactively embracing change in the future, listing strategies you can employ.

Adaptability is not just a survival skill; it's a key driver of success in today's rapidly changing world. By learning from the eagle's ability to adapt to shifting conditions, you can navigate uncertainty with confidence, seize new opportunities, and thrive in a dynamic environment. Just as eagles soar effortlessly in changing winds, your adaptability will enable you to reach new heights in your personal and professional journey.

Chapter 2:
Reaching New Heights - Soaring

Lesson 3 - Visionary Leadership

Eagles' Perspective: Inspiring Visionary Leadership

Visionary leadership is the compass that guides organizations and individuals toward a future brimming with possibilities. Eagles, with their ability to see from great heights, offer a striking metaphor for visionary leadership. In this lesson, we'll explore how eagles' extraordinary vision aligns with visionary leadership, discover leaders who have transformed their organizations through this approach, and provide a comprehensive action plan to help you develop and communicate a compelling vision.

Eagles' Vision and Visionary Leadership

- ✓ Seeing the Bigger Picture: Eagles' elevated vantage points provide them with a comprehensive view of their surroundings. Similarly, visionary leaders possess the ability to see beyond the immediate challenges and grasp the bigger picture, identifying opportunities and potential obstacles.
- ✓ Long-Term Perspective: Eagles' flights at great heights parallel the long-term focus of visionary leaders. They are not swayed by short-term fluctuations but maintain a steadfast commitment to their overarching vision.
- ✓ Inspiring Others: Eagles' vision is not just for their own benefit; it aids them in hunting, protecting their territory, and nurturing their young. Visionary leaders inspire and mobilize

their teams by sharing a compelling vision that aligns with a greater purpose.

Leaders Who Transformed Organizations Through Visionary Leadership

Example 1: *Martin Luther King Jr.:* Martin Luther King Jr. is an iconic example of a visionary leader who transformed society. His "I Have a Dream" speech articulated a vision of racial equality and justice in America. His unwavering commitment to this vision played a pivotal role in the civil rights movement and led to significant legislative changes.

Example 2: *Elon Musk:* Elon Musk's visionary leadership has had a profound impact on multiple industries. He founded SpaceX with a vision of making humanity a multi-planetary species and Tesla to accelerate the transition to sustainable energy. Musk's relentless pursuit of these visions has driven innovation in space exploration and electric vehicles.

Action Plan: Steps to Develop and Communicate a Compelling Vision

Self-Reflection and Clarity:

- ✓ Reflect on your personal values and aspirations to identify what truly matters to you.
- ✓ Clarify your vision for your organization or personal goals, considering the long-term impact.

Engage Your Team:

- ✓ Involve your team members in shaping the vision. Encourage their input and insights.
- ✓ Ensure alignment between individual and organizational visions.

Craft a Vivid Vision Statement:

- ✓ Create a concise and inspiring vision statement that encapsulates your aspirations.
- ✓ Use clear and vivid language that paints a picture of the desired future.

Lead by Example:

- ✓ Demonstrate your commitment to the vision through your actions and decisions.
- ✓ Set a high standard of behavior and work ethic to inspire others.

Effective Communication:

- ✓ Regularly communicate the vision to your team, using various channels and formats.
- ✓ Share stories and examples that illustrate how the vision will positively impact the organization and its stakeholders.

Measure Progress and Adapt:

- ✓ Establish key performance indicators (KPIs) to track progress toward the vision.
- ✓ Be open to revisiting and refining the vision as circumstances evolve.

Empower and Delegate:

- ✓ Delegate tasks and responsibilities that align with the vision to capable team members.
- ✓ Empower your team to take ownership and contribute to achieving the vision.

It's your turn! Put this into real action now!

Exercise 3: Vision Statement Creation

- ✓ Craft a clear and concise personal or organizational vision statement.
- ✓ Share it with your team or colleagues and solicit their feedback.
- ✓ Consider how this vision aligns with your daily decisions and actions.

- ✓ Develop a list of actionable steps to communicate and reinforce this vision in your leadership role.

Visionary leadership is a powerful force for transformation. By drawing inspiration from the eagle's perspective and learning from visionary leaders who have left indelible marks on history, you can chart a course towards a brighter future. Your ability to develop and communicate a compelling vision will guide your organization or personal endeavors to new heights of success and significance.

Lesson 4 - Persistence

Eagles' Tenacity: The Power of Persistence

Persistence is the unwavering determination to pursue one's goals despite obstacles and setbacks. Eagles exemplify this trait in their relentless pursuit of prey and their ability to navigate adverse weather conditions. In this chapter, we'll delve into how eagles' persistence relates to human determination, share stories of individuals who achieved remarkable success through their unyielding persistence, and provide a comprehensive action plan to help you cultivate this invaluable trait.

Eagles' Persistence and Its Parallel to Human Determination

- ✓ Relentless Pursuit: Eagles are known for their relentless pursuit of prey. They maintain focus and tenacity, adapting their tactics as needed to secure their meal. Similarly, human determination involves a relentless pursuit of goals, even in the face of challenges.
- ✓ Adversity Resilience: Eagles demonstrate the ability to navigate adverse weather conditions such as storms. This parallels the human need to persist through life's storms, whether they are personal or professional hardships.
- ✓ Long-Term Commitment: Eagles' persistence extends to the long term. They commit to nurturing their young and protecting their territory throughout their lives. Likewise, human determination often involves a long-term commitment to achieving significant goals.

Achieving Remarkable Success Through Persistence

Example 1: *Thomas Edison:* Thomas Edison's pursuit of the electric light bulb is a testament to persistence. He conducted thousands of experiments over several years before successfully inventing the practical incandescent light bulb. His famous quote, "I have not failed. I've just found 10,000 ways that won't work," reflects his unyielding determination.

Example 2: *J.K. Rowling:* J.K. Rowling, the author of the Harry Potter series, faced numerous rejections from publishers before finding success. Her persistence in pursuing her dream of becoming a published author eventually led to one of the most successful book series in history.

Action Plan: Strategies to Cultivate Unwavering Determination

Set Clear and Meaningful Goals:

- ✓ Define your goals with clarity, ensuring they are aligned with your values and aspirations.
- ✓ Understand why these goals matter to you on a personal level.

Build Resilience:

- ✓ Develop emotional resilience to bounce back from setbacks.
- ✓ Maintain a growth mindset, viewing challenges as opportunities for learning and growth.

Break It Down:

- ✓ Divide large goals into smaller, manageable milestones.
- ✓ Celebrate your achievements along the way to maintain motivation.

Stay Focused:

- ✓ Minimize distractions and stay focused on your goals.
- ✓ Create a conducive work environment that supports your persistence.

Seek Support and Mentorship:

- ✓ Surround yourself with a supportive network of friends, family, or mentors.
- ✓ Seek guidance from those who have achieved similar goals.

Continuous Learning:

- ✓ Invest in acquiring new skills and knowledge that are relevant to your goals.
- ✓ Stay up-to-date with industry trends and best practices.

Visualize Success:

- ✓ Regularly visualize yourself achieving your goals.
- ✓ Use this mental imagery to reinforce your determination and motivation.

It's your turn! Put this into real action now!
Exercise 4: Goal Persistence Challenge

- ✓ Identify a challenging long-term goal you have set for yourself.
- ✓ Break it down into smaller, manageable milestones.
- ✓ Create a visual representation of your goal and milestones, such as a progress chart.
- ✓ Commit to achieving a specific milestone within a set timeframe, and track your progress diligently.

Persistence is the driving force behind many great achievements. By drawing inspiration from the tenacity of eagles and learning from individuals who have achieved remarkable success through their unwavering determination, you can cultivate this essential trait. As you embark on your journey to reach your goals, remember that persistence is the key to overcoming challenges and ultimately realizing your dreams.

Chapter 3:
Unyielding Strength - Strength

Lesson 5 - Resilience

Eagles' Endurance: The Power of Resilience

Resilience is the ability to bounce back from adversity, to endure and overcome life's challenges. Eagles, with their capacity to endure harsh conditions like storms, provide a powerful metaphor for resilience. In this chapter, we will explore how eagles' resilience relates to human strength in the face of adversity, share stories of individuals who triumphed over setbacks through resilience, and provide a comprehensive action plan to help you build resilience in your own life.

Eagles' Resilience and Its Parallel to Human Strength

- ✓ Endurance Through Adversity: Eagles, while majestic in flight, also endure challenging conditions such as storms. They use their strength and resilience to navigate through adversity and emerge unscathed. Similarly, humans need resilience to withstand life's storms, which may include personal, professional, or health-related challenges.
- ✓ Adaptability in the Face of Change: Eagles adapt to changing weather conditions and unforeseen challenges during their hunting and nesting processes. This adaptability mirrors the human capacity to adapt to new circumstances and pivot when necessary.
- ✓ Long-Term Commitment: Eagles display long-term commitment to their nests and families. They repair and rebuild their nests year after year, demonstrating persistence and resilience. Similarly, humans often need

resilience to sustain their commitments and goals over time.

Overcoming Setbacks Through Resilience

Example 1*: Oprah Winfrey:* Oprah Winfrey's journey from a troubled childhood to becoming one of the most influential women in media is a testament to resilience. She overcame personal hardships, including abuse and poverty, to build an empire based on empowerment and inspiration.

Example 2: *Nelson Mandela:* Nelson Mandela's 27-year imprisonment for his anti-apartheid activism could have embittered many, but he emerged from incarceration with a remarkable level of forgiveness, resilience, and determination. His ability to lead South Africa toward reconciliation and democracy reflects the power of resilience.

Action Plan: Techniques to Build Resilience in the Face of Challenges

Embrace Adversity as a Learning Opportunity:

- ✓ Reframe challenges as opportunities for personal growth and learning.
- ✓ Maintain a growth mindset, believing that you can develop resilience.

Strengthen Your Support Network:

- ✓ Cultivate relationships with friends, family, and mentors who can provide emotional support.
- ✓ Seek professional help when needed, such as therapy or counseling.

Mindfulness and Stress Management:

- ✓ Practice mindfulness techniques, such as meditation or deep breathing exercises, to manage stress.

- ✓ Develop healthy coping mechanisms to deal with stress and anxiety.

Set Realistic Goals:

- ✓ Establish achievable goals and expectations to avoid undue stress.
- ✓ Break larger goals into smaller, manageable steps to maintain a sense of progress.

Adaptive Thinking:

- ✓ Challenge negative thought patterns and replace them with more positive and constructive thinking.
- ✓ Develop problem-solving skills to navigate challenges effectively.

Physical Well-Being:

- ✓ Maintain a healthy lifestyle through regular exercise, balanced nutrition, and sufficient rest.
- ✓ Physical health is closely linked to emotional and mental resilience.

Seek Meaning and Purpose:

- ✓ Connect with your values and passions to find a sense of purpose that can sustain you through adversity.
- ✓ Understand the "why" behind your actions and goals.

It's your turn! Put this into real action now!

Exercise 5: Resilience Boosting Routine

- ✓ Develop a daily resilience routine that includes activities like mindfulness meditation, exercise, or journaling.
- ✓ Commit to practicing this routine for a month.
- ✓ Reflect on how it impacts your ability to handle stress and setbacks.

- ✓ Adjust and refine your routine based on what works best for you.

Resilience is a foundational trait that empowers individuals to withstand and overcome life's trials. By drawing inspiration from the enduring spirit of eagles and learning from individuals who have triumphed over adversity, you can cultivate this essential trait. As you build resilience in your own life, you will be better equipped to navigate challenges and emerge stronger, just as eagles soar higher after enduring storms.

Lesson 6 - Teamwork

Eagles' Collaboration: The Power of Teamwork

Teamwork is the cornerstone of success in both the natural world and the realms of business and leadership. Eagles, known for their collaborative hunting pairs or families, provide a compelling example of teamwork. In this chapter, we will delve into the collaborative nature of eagle hunting, present case studies of successful teams in business and leadership, and provide a comprehensive action plan to help you build effective teams and foster collaboration.

Eagle Hunting Pairs and Family Collaboration

- ✓ Collaborative Hunting: Eagles often hunt in pairs, where one bird flushes out prey, and the other captures it. This division of labor maximizes their chances of success. Additionally, eagle families work together to raise and protect their young, emphasizing the importance of cooperation.
- ✓ Effective Communication: Eagles communicate effectively during hunting, using non-verbal cues and coordinated actions. Their communication is essential for a successful hunt.
- ✓ Shared Responsibility: Each member of an eagle hunting pair or family has a specific role and responsibilities, contributing to the overall success of the group.

Case Studies of Successful Teams in Business and Leadership

Example 1: *Apple Inc:* Apple Inc. is known for its successful cross-functional teams. Steve Jobs, the co-founder, emphasized the importance of collaboration and diversity in teams. The development of the iPhone, for instance, involved engineers, designers, and marketers working together closely to create a groundbreaking product.
Example 2: *Apollo 11 Moon Landing Team:* The Apollo 11 mission that landed humans on the moon was a remarkable example of teamwork. Scientists, engineers, astronauts, and support staff from various organizations, including NASA, worked together to achieve this historic feat.

Action Plan: Building Effective Teams and Fostering Collaboration

Clear Roles and Goals:

- ✓ Define clear roles and responsibilities for team members.
- ✓ Establish specific, measurable goals that align with the team's mission.

Effective Communication:

- ✓ Foster open and transparent communication within the team.
- ✓ Use tools and technologies that facilitate collaboration, such as project management software and video conferencing.

Diversity and Inclusion:

- ✓ Build teams with diverse backgrounds, skills, and perspectives.
- ✓ Create an inclusive environment where all team members feel valued and heard.

Conflict Resolution:

- ✓ Develop conflict resolution strategies to address disagreements constructively.

- ✓ Encourage healthy debate and diverse opinions while maintaining a focus on shared goals.

Empowerment and Autonomy:

- ✓ Provide team members with the autonomy to make decisions within their areas of responsibility.
- ✓ Empower individuals to take ownership of their work and contribute ideas.

Continuous Improvement:

- ✓ Encourage a culture of continuous learning and improvement.
- ✓ Regularly evaluate team performance and seek feedback for enhancement.

Recognition and Reward:

- ✓ Acknowledge and reward individual and team achievements.
- ✓ Celebrate milestones and successes together to build team morale.

It's your turn! Put this into real action now!

Exercise 6: Team Building Simulation

- ✓ Create a hypothetical team challenge or project.
- ✓ Invite a group of colleagues or team members to participate.
- ✓ Assign roles, set objectives, and encourage collaboration.
- ✓ Debrief the experience and discuss what worked well and what could be improved in terms of teamwork.

Teamwork is the bedrock of achievement in organizations and projects. By studying the collaborative nature of eagle hunting pairs and families and drawing inspiration from successful teams in various domains, you can develop the skills and strategies needed to build effective teams and foster collaboration. A well-coordinated team, like a pair of eagles working in tandem, can achieve extraordinary results and overcome challenges with grace and efficiency.

Chapter 4:

Navigating Life's Storms - Lessons in Adversity

Lesson 7 - Embracing Failure

Eagles' Resilience: The Wisdom of Embracing Failure

Embracing failure is a critical aspect of personal and professional growth. Eagles provide valuable lessons in this regard through their ability to learn from unsuccessful hunting attempts. In this chapter, we will explore how eagles' response to failure can teach us resilience, share stories of business leaders who turned failures into opportunities, and provide a comprehensive action plan to help you develop a growth mindset in the face of failure.

Eagles' Response to Failure

- ✓ Adaptive Learning: Eagles do not become discouraged by failed hunting attempts. Instead, they adapt their strategies, learning from their mistakes and improving their chances of success in future hunts.
- ✓ Perseverance: Eagles demonstrate perseverance by continuing their efforts until they achieve their goal. They do not give up easily but persistently pursue their prey, even if initial attempts are unsuccessful.
- ✓ Resilience: Eagles maintain their physical and mental resilience, ensuring that setbacks do not deter them from their ultimate objective – securing food for survival.

Business Leaders Who Turned Failure into Opportunity

Example 1: *Steve Jobs (Apple):* Steve Jobs faced numerous failures and setbacks throughout his career, including being ousted from Apple, the company he co-founded. However, he returned to Apple years later, and his leadership transformed the company into one of the most successful technology companies in the world. His ability to learn from failure and turn it into innovation is evident in products like the iPod, iPhone, and iPad.

Example 2: *Henry Ford:* Before founding the Ford Motor Company, Henry Ford experienced multiple business failures, including two failed car companies. However, he used these failures as learning experiences, leading to the development of the affordable Model T and revolutionizing the automobile industry.

Action Plan: Developing a Growth Mindset in the Face of Failure

Reframe Failure as a Learning Opportunity:

- ✓ Change your perspective on failure, viewing it as a chance to learn and grow.
- ✓ Understand that mistakes are a natural part of the learning process.

Set Realistic Expectations:

- ✓ Avoid setting unrealistically high standards for yourself or your team.
- ✓ Recognize that failure is an inherent part of setting ambitious goals.

Continuous Improvement:

- ✓ Commit to ongoing improvement and development in both personal and professional aspects.
- ✓ Seek feedback and use it constructively to make adjustments.

Resilience Building:

- ✓ Develop emotional resilience to handle the emotional impact of failure.
- ✓ Cultivate the ability to bounce back quickly from setbacks.

Embrace Risk-Taking:

- ✓ Be open to taking calculated risks in pursuit of your goals.
- ✓ Understand that some risks may lead to failure but also present opportunities for growth.

Learn from Failure:

- ✓ Conduct a post-mortem analysis of failed projects or initiatives.
- ✓ Identify specific lessons learned and apply them to future endeavors.

Encourage a Growth Mindset in Teams:

- ✓ Promote a culture that values innovation and experimentation.
- ✓ Create an environment where team members feel safe to take risks and learn from failure.

It's your turn! Put this into real action now!
Exercise 7: Failure Reflection Practice

- ✓ Choose a recent failure or setback you've experienced.
- ✓ Reflect on the specific lessons you've learned from this failure.
- ✓ Identify how you can apply these lessons to future endeavors.
- ✓ Share your failure story and insights with a colleague or mentor.

Embracing failure as a stepping stone to success is a hallmark of resilience and growth. By observing eagles' ability to learn from unsuccessful hunting attempts and drawing inspiration from leaders who turned failures into opportunities, you can develop a growth mindset that empowers you to thrive in the face of adversity. Failure is not a roadblock but a detour on the path to achievement, and with the right mindset, it can lead to even greater success.

Lesson 8 - Leadership by Example

Eagles' Guiding Light: The Art of Leadership by Example

Leading by example is a cornerstone of effective leadership, both in nature and in the world of business and leadership. Eagles, through their actions in guiding and nurturing their young, provide a compelling illustration of leadership by example. In this chapter, we will explore how eagles lead their young through their actions, showcase leaders who set positive examples, and provide a comprehensive action plan to help you become a role model and inspire others through your actions.

Eagles' Leadership by Example

- ✓ Demonstrative Parenting: Eagles lead by example in their role as parents. They demonstrate hunting techniques, provide food, and protect their young, teaching them essential survival skills through their actions.
- ✓ Protection and Safety: Eagles' vigilant protection of their offspring and their nests serves as a model of care and safety. They shield their young from predators and adverse weather conditions.
- ✓ Steadfastness: Eagles exhibit steadfast commitment to their families and territory, leading by example in their persistence, resilience, and loyalty.

Leaders Who Set Positive Examples

***Example 1**: Mahatma Gandhi:* Mahatma Gandhi, a leader of India's nonviolent independence movement, is renowned for his commitment to peaceful resistance and social justice. His actions, including peaceful protests and fasting, inspired millions and led to India's independence from British rule.

Example 2: *Angela Merkel:* Angela Merkel, the former Chancellor of Germany, is recognized for her calm and steady leadership, particularly during challenging times such as the European financial crisis and the refugee crisis. Her leadership style emphasized rational decision-making and diplomacy.

Action Plan: Becoming a Role Model and Inspiring Others Through Your Actions

Clarity of Values and Principles:

- ✓ Define your core values and principles that will guide your actions and decisions.
- ✓ Ensure alignment between your values and your leadership style.

Lead with Integrity:

- ✓ Act consistently with your values and principles, even when facing difficult choices.
- ✓ Be honest, transparent, and ethical in all your interactions.

Effective Communication:

- ✓ Clearly articulate your vision and expectations to your team or followers.
- ✓ Maintain open lines of communication, actively listening to others' perspectives.

Empower Others:

- ✓ Delegate responsibility and authority to team members, allowing them to take ownership of their tasks.
- ✓ Encourage autonomy and initiative, fostering a sense of empowerment.

Consistency:

- ✓ Consistency in your actions and decisions builds trust and reliability.
- ✓ Avoid contradictory behavior that may undermine your leadership.

Accountability:

- ✓ Hold yourself accountable for your actions and decisions.
- ✓ Acknowledge mistakes and take corrective measures when necessary.

Continuous Learning:

- ✓ Demonstrate a commitment to personal and professional growth.
- ✓ Encourage a culture of learning and improvement within your team or organization.

It's your turn! Put this into real action now!
Exercise 8: Values Integration Challenge

- ✓ List your core values as a leader.
- ✓ Select one value to focus on each week.
- ✓ Document specific actions and behaviors that align with this value.
- ✓ Seek feedback from team members on how they perceive your consistency in embodying this value.

Leadership by example is a powerful tool for inspiring and motivating others. By observing eagles' guidance to their young and drawing inspiration from leaders who set positive examples, you can develop the qualities and strategies needed to become a role model in your own sphere of influence. Your actions and values can inspire others to follow in your footsteps and contribute to a more positive and successful environment.

Action Plan to Implement these Lessons Daily

Implementing the lessons from the previous chapters into daily life as a business leader requires deliberate effort and commitment. Here is a detailed action plan for business leaders to practice and apply these lessons daily, making them an integral part of their leadership system:

1. Visionary Leadership:

Define and Communicate Your Vision:

- ✓ Set aside time daily to clarify and refine your personal and organizational vision.
- ✓ Create a concise vision statement that you can easily communicate to your team.

Align Actions with Vision:

- ✓ Before making decisions, ask yourself if they align with your vision and long-term goals.
- ✓ Continuously evaluate and adjust your strategies to stay on course.

Inspire and Motivate:

- ✓ Regularly communicate your vision to your team through meetings, emails, and one-on-one conversations.
- ✓ Share success stories that exemplify how your vision is being realized.

2. Teamwork:

Foster Collaboration:

- ✓ Encourage open communication and collaboration among team members.
- ✓ Lead by example by actively seeking input and feedback from your team.

Build Diverse Teams:

- ✓ Ensure your teams consist of individuals with diverse backgrounds, skills, and perspectives.
- ✓ Emphasize the value of diversity and inclusion within your organization.

Empower Your Team:

- ✓ Delegate responsibility and decision-making authority to team members.
- ✓ Create a culture where team members feel empowered to take ownership of their tasks.

3. Persistence:

Set Daily Goals:

- ✓ Begin each day by setting clear and achievable daily goals.
- ✓ Maintain focus on completing these goals despite distractions.

Embrace Setbacks as Opportunities:

- ✓ Reframe setbacks as opportunities for learning and improvement.
- ✓ Use challenges as stepping stones toward your long-term objectives.

Maintain a Growth Mindset:

- ✓ Cultivate a mindset that embraces persistence and continuous improvement.
- ✓ View difficulties as a natural part of your journey toward success.

4. Resilience:

Practice Stress Management:

- ✓ Incorporate stress-reduction techniques into your daily routine, such as mindfulness or exercise.
- ✓ Recognize the signs of stress and take proactive steps to address them.

Build a Support Network:

- ✓ Develop relationships with mentors, peers, and friends who can provide emotional support.
- ✓ Seek professional guidance when needed to enhance your resilience.

Maintain a Positive Perspective:

- ✓ Focus on solutions rather than dwelling on problems.
- ✓ Celebrate small victories and maintain optimism in the face of challenges.

5. Embracing Failure:

Experiment Regularly:

- ✓ Encourage a culture of experimentation within your organization.
- ✓ Lead by example by trying new approaches and being open to potential failures.

Learn and Adapt:

- ✓ After experiencing a setback or failure, conduct a post-mortem analysis to extract lessons.
- ✓ Apply these lessons to refine your strategies and decision-making.

Normalize Failure:

- ✓ Share your own failures and how you learned from them with your team.
- ✓ Create an environment where failure is seen as a step toward success rather than a defeat.

6. Leadership by Example:

Model the Behavior You Expect:

- ✓ Consistently demonstrate the values, work ethic, and behavior you expect from your team.
- ✓ Be a role model for professionalism, integrity, and ethical conduct.

Connect with Your Team:

- ✓ Develop personal connections with team members through regular conversations and active listening.
- ✓ Show genuine care and interest in their well-being and growth.

Acknowledge and Celebrate Success:

- ✓ Recognize and celebrate both individual and team achievements.
- ✓ Express gratitude and appreciation for your team's contributions.

Remember that consistency and persistence are key to making these lessons a part of your daily life as a business leader. It may take time to fully integrate these practices, but the long-term benefits in terms of leadership effectiveness and organizational success are well worth the effort. By following this action plan and staying committed to personal growth, you can become a more effective and inspiring leader in your organization.

Conclusion

In the soaring journey through the pages of "Soaring to Success: Lessons from the Eagle for Business and Leadership," we have traversed the skies alongside one of nature's most majestic creatures—the eagle. With each lesson drawn from the eagle's world, we have ventured deeper into the heart of leadership, personal growth, and the pursuit of excellence.

As we conclude this enlightening exploration, let us reflect on the profound wisdom we have gleaned from these remarkable birds of prey. The eagle, with its swiftness, height, and strength, has been our guide and mentor, offering valuable insights into the qualities that elevate leaders and individuals to greater heights.

We have learned that visionary leadership begins with a clear vision and a commitment to inspiring others. We have seen how teamwork transforms ordinary efforts into extraordinary achievements, fostering collaboration and unity within organizations.

The lessons of persistence have reminded us that resilience in the face of adversity is the hallmark of those who dare to dream big. Embracing failure has unveiled the hidden opportunities within setbacks, encouraging us to see challenges as stepping stones to success.

Finally, we have explored the transformative power of leadership by example—how the actions and behaviors of leaders shape the culture and success of their organizations.

As we bid farewell to our avian mentors, let us carry these lessons in our hearts and minds, for they are not just words on a page but a blueprint for a life well-lived. The eagle teaches us that greatness is not a destination but a continuous journey—a journey marked by growth, adaptability, and the unyielding pursuit of our full potential.

Now, it is your turn to take flight, to embrace these lessons and make them a part of your leadership and personal philosophy. Let them be the wind beneath your wings as you rise above challenges and soar to new horizons. Let them guide your decisions, inspire your actions, and transform your leadership style.

Remember that the path to success is not without its storms and trials, but with the wisdom of the eagle as your guide, you can navigate even the most turbulent skies with grace and determination.

In closing, "Soaring to Success" is not just a book; it is a call to action—a call to become the leader you were meant to be, to excel in every facet of life, and to embrace the extraordinary potential within you.

So, spread your wings and soar, for the journey to success is a lifelong adventure, and the eagle's lessons will be with you every step of the way.

About the Author 'GERARD ASSEY'

Gerard Assey is a Graduate in Economics, a PGD in Management (HRD) and holds a Doctorate in Leadership. Gerard holds several International Qualifications in Sales, Debt Collection, Training & Teaching, and is a 'Fellow' of the prestigious 'Institute of Sales & Marketing Management'-UK, a Certified NLP Practitioner, a 'Certified Trainer', an 'Accredited Management Teacher-Behavioral Sciences', a 'Certified Competency Facilitator', a 'Certified Management Consultant'- (the International credentials of a professional management consultant, awarded in accordance with global standards of the ICMCI); and a Certification from the University of Michigan in 'Successful Negotiation: Essential Strategies and Skills'

He is also a Member of the 'National Association of Sales Professionals' backed with several years experience in varied industries, both in India and Overseas. He also holds an 'Etiquette Consultant' Certification from the USA (by Sue Fox, Author of Best Seller: 'Business Etiquette for Dummies'. She has trained some of the top celebrities' world over). He was also a recipient of a scholarship for extensive training in Japan on 'Corporate Management for India'.

Gerard Assey is 'Founder & Chief Corporate Trainer' of the Group: **'Citius, Altius, Fortius Unlimited'**- an organization that **celebrated 20 years of Glorious Service** in 2021, focusing on 3 Core Competencies:

People. Performance. Profit; in functional areas of Sales & Marketing, HR & Organizational Development, covering Recruitment, Training & Consultancy!

Having managed organizations with large Sales Forces in India & Overseas, his specialization cover extensive areas of Sales Training (All levels - Presentation, Negotiation, Key/ Strategic Accounts Management & Managerial Skills for all sectors), Bid Proposal/ Capture Planning/ Management Trainings, Retail Sales, Customer Service & Customer Retention Programs, Training for Prevention & Collection of Debt, Self & Personal Development Programs (Time Management, Teamwork & Team Building, Business Etiquette & Personal Grooming, Leadership & Managerial Skills, People Management Skills, Train-the-Trainer etc), including preparation of Custom-designed Business Manuals for Internal (HR, Induction, and Sales etc) & External use (Instruction, User Manuals).

Gerard has successfully conducted over 6000 Trainings & Workshops (as of Oct '23) all across India, Middle East, Africa, Europe & S.E. Asia. Besides public programs conducted regularly, both in India & Overseas, he has some of the top names as clients whom he services from Single Owners to large Public & Government undertakings, covering all sectors, for their in-house needs.

His website: www.CollectionSkills.com is the only one in this part of the world to be featured in the 'Collections & Credit Risk Magazine-USA' under 'Who's Who in Training' and ranks TOP, along with other websites listed below on most search engines.

Gerard is author of 89 books already (Nov 2023),

A few of our business related books:

1. Bite-sized Bits on Commonsense Management
2. Heart to Heart on Life's Principles'
3. How to become a Successful Manager
4. The Sales Professionals' Master Workbook of S.Y.S.T.E.M.S
5. The Professional Business Email Etiquette Handbook & Guide
6. The Professional Business Video-Conferencing Etiquette Handbook & Guide
7. Professional Presentation Skills
8. Exceptional Customer Service
9. Professional Tele-Marketing Skills
10. Professional Debt Collection Skills
11. The G.R.E.A.T. Sales & Service Workbook
12. Sales Training Advantage for Results (*The Ultimate Sales Training Manual to enable you stand out as a S.T.A.R.*)
13. CEO Daily Planner & Organizer
14. The Sales Professionals' Master Daily Planner
15. The Professional Debt Collector's Master Daily Planner
16. My Daily Planner & Organizer
17. MY EMERGENCY INFORMATION RECORD (Family Emergency & Peace of Mind Planner)
18. The Ultimate Therapist & Counselors Planner and Organizer
19. Building an Ethical Workplace
20. Managing Relationships at Work
21. Managing Business Meetings Effectively
22. Effective Delegation Skills
23. Goal Setting for Success
24. B2B Selling by Email
25. Professional Business Etiquette & Grooming
26. Dining Etiquette & Table Manners
27. Effective Networking Skills
28. Grooming, Etiquette & Manners for Teens, Young Adults & Future Leaders
29. Inter-Personal Skills
30. Get Ready, Get Hired!
31. Selling in a Recession
32. Effective Receivables Management in an Economic Downturn!
33. Real Estate & Property Sales Training

34. Credit Sales & Accounts Receivable Management
35. Selling Skills for Real Estate & Property Advisors
36. Take G.R.E.A.T. C.A.R.E!
37. Spa, Salon & Health Club Selling Skills
38. Selling Travel, Holiday & MICE Services
39. Selling Skills for Spa's, Salons & Health Clubs
40. Retailing in Salons & Spas
41. Selling Holiday, Vacation, Tours & Packages
42. The Power of Sales Referrals
43. Selling Luxury
44. Technical Selling Skills
45. Financial Advisors Sales Training
46. Dealing with Burnout at Work Monopolize Your Markets
47. Selling to Affluent Customers
48. Growing up with Grace
49. Financial Selling Skills
50. *The Effective Manager's Guide: Key Skills to Thrive*
51. From Aspiring to Inspiring: A Guide for New Managers on the Rise
52. The Power of Focus
53. Selling with Integrity: Sell Like Jesus The Perfect Role Model!
54. 31 Habits of Champions: Your 31-Day Journey to Greatness
55. Rejecting Grasshopper Talk: From Grasshopper to Giant-Killer-*Defeating Giants Daily!*
56. Navigate the AI-Powered Future of Bid & Proposals: Up-Skill to Stay Relevant with Alternative Career Paths & Opportunities
57. Hiring Sales Winners
58. Present with Impact
59. Success Unlocked: *Breaking Free from Habits that Hold You Back*
60. Complaints to Cheers, Feedback to Gold: Mastering Complaints Management
61. Thriving Together: *Cultivating Diversity, Equity, and Inclusion*
62. Coaching Skills for Sales Managers
63. Soaring to Success in Business & Leadership: Swifter, Higher, Stronger!

Besides regularly contributing to business & trade journals, including international ones such as the 'Creative Training Techniques' and the 'Sales News' of the U.S.A, He is also a member of several prestigious bodies & trade associations, having participated in many Conferences & Workshops in India & Overseas.

Prior to his last assignment of leading & managing a large MNC as head, Gerard had a 3-year stint in the Middle East as a Consultant with a leading British Consultancy Firm.

As the past 'Official Country Representative' for the International Business Award- 'THE STEVIES'-(the business world's own Oscar) for about 4 years- he ensured a few Indian companies that qualify for the same every year!

Gerard can be contacted at:
Email: training@Sales-Training.in,training@CollectionSkills.com
Websites:

www.Sales-Training.in
www.EtiquetteWorks.in
www.CollectionSkills.com
www.RetailSalesTraining.in
www.SalesTrainingIndia.com
www.ManualPreparation.com
www.TrainingWithPuppets.com
www.FirstContactAcademy.com
www.SalesAndMarketingRecruiter.com

Our TRAININGS that can help your team

- ✓ **Sales Effectiveness**: Selling Skills for any Sector: Service/ Logistics/ FMCG Realty/ Insurance & Finance/ Media/ SPA's, Health Clubs & Salons/ Key Account Management, Effective Negotiation Skills/ Bid & Proposal Management Skills/ Retail Sales Training: Any Sector (Auto, Jewelry, Clothing, Luxury etc)
- ✓ **Customer Service Skills**-Complaints Handling & Customer Retention
- ✓ **Debt Prevention & Collection Skills**
- ✓ **Etiquette & Grooming**
- ✓ **Leadership & Managerial Skills**
- ✓ **Self & Personal Development Skills**: Presentation Skills/ Effective Communication Skills/Business Proposal Writing Skills/ Problem Solving & Decision Making Skills/ Empowering Secretaries-The perfect PA! (For Secretaries & PA's)/ Effective Time Management/ Teamwork & Teambuilding/ P.R.I.D.E- **P**ersonal **R**esponsibility **I**n **D**elivering **E**xcellence

www.ingramcontent.com/pod-product-compliance
Lightning Source LLC
Chambersburg PA
CBHW062113160726
48282CB00026B/787
9789392492990